Fast Facts About Insects & Spiders

Fast Facts About
BUTTERFLIES

by Lisa J. Amstutz

Raintree is an imprint of Capstone Global Library Limited, a company incorporated in England and Wales having its registered office at 264 Banbury Road, Oxford, OX2 7DY – Registered company number: 6695582

www.raintree.co.uk
myorders@raintree.co.uk

Edited by Abby Huff
Designed by Kyle Grenz
Original illustrations © Capstone Global Library Limited 2022
Picture research by Jo Miller
Production by Tori Abraham
Originated by Capstone Global Library Ltd

978 1 3982 1326 5 (hardback)
978 1 3982 1325 8 (paperback)

British Library Cataloguing in Publication Data
A full catalogue record for this book is available from the British Library.

Acknowledgements
We would like to thank the following for permission to reproduce photographs: Shutterstock: Brian Lasenby, 6, Cathy Keifer, 16, 17, Cornel Constantin, 10, Eric Isselee, cover, Gokula Priya Eswaran, 9, Inspiration GP, 20 (left), jakrit yuenprakhon, 14, JHVEPhoto, 19, jonathan_law, 5, Ken Griffiths, 13, liu yangjun, 20 (clothespin), Malgorzata Wryk-Igras, 21, marla dawn studio, 20 (bottom middle), Mega Pixel, 20 (top right), Peaw_GT, 11, Petr Ganaj, 7, Raafi Nur Ali, 15, riphoto3, 20 (bottom right), Russell Marshall, 8, SweetLemons, 20 (eyes), Wansfordphoto, 18, zabavina (background), cover and throughout

Every effort has been made to contact copyright holders of material reproduced in this book. Any omissions will be rectified in subsequent printings if notice is given to the publisher.

All the internet addresses (URLs) given in this book were valid at the time of going to press. However, due to the dynamic nature of the internet, some addresses may have changed, or sites may have changed or ceased to exist since publication. While the author and publisher regret any inconvenience this may cause readers, no responsibility for any such changes can be accepted by either the author or the publisher.

Printed and bound in India.

Conte

Words in **bold** are in the glossary.

All about butterflies

Butterflies are **insects**. A butterfly has six legs. It also has three body sections. Can you see the two long **antennae** on its head? They can sniff out food. Each one has a bulb at the end.

wings

antennae

legs

A butterfly has four wings. The wings have tiny scales. These pieces shine when light hits them. They give the wings colour.

A close-up of a monarch butterfly's wing

Butterflies come in many colours. Some blend in with plants. This helps butterflies hide. Others have bright colours or big spots. This warns enemies to stay away.

Queen Alexandra's birdwing is the largest butterfly in the world.

There are more than 17,000 types of butterflies. They can be as big as a dinner plate! They can be as small as your fingernail.

Butterflies live all over the world. They live in forests. They live in hot deserts and on cold mountains. But they do not live in Antarctica. It is too cold there!

Time to eat

A butterfly's mouth is like a straw. It is very long. It curls up when it's not in use. The insect stretches it out to drink.

Many butterflies drink **nectar**. It is a sweet liquid from flowers. They also drink from mud puddles. They get salts and **minerals** there. This keeps them healthy.

Butterflies help plants. They **pollinate** flowers. A butterfly lands on a flower. It reaches in for nectar. A powder from the flower sticks to its body. This is pollen. The insect goes to a new flower. The pollen brushes off. Now fruit and seeds can grow.

A butterfly's life

A female butterfly lands on a leaf. She uses her feet to taste it. Is it the right type of plant for her young to eat? Yes! She lays her eggs here.

egg

A **larva** hatches out of each egg. It is also called a caterpillar. It eats the leaf. It grows. Soon it sheds its skin (**moults**). It will moult four or more times. Each time it gets bigger.

Finally, the larva makes a case around itself. The case is called a **pupa** or chrysalis. Inside, the larva's body changes. It may take a few weeks. Some stay inside for years.

A larva making a pupa

A butterfly leaving the pupa

The butterfly is ready. It breaks out of the case. Its wings are wet. It slowly flaps them. The wings dry. Now it can fly away.

Fun facts

- Butterflies and moths are related, but they are not the same. Moth antennae are feathery. They feed at night. Butterflies eat during the day.

- The glasswing butterfly has clear wings. You can see through them!

glasswing butterfly

Monarch butterflies in Mexico during winter

- The monarch butterfly flies south in winter. It can travel up to 4,828 kilometres (3,000 miles).

- Some butterflies feed on animal poo!

Build a butterfly

What you need:

- felt-tips or watercolour paints
- coffee filter
- clothes peg
- half a pipe cleaner
- two googly eyes
- glue

What to do:

1. Draw or paint a pattern on the coffee filter. This will make the wings. Let it dry.

2. Pinch the middle of the filter together. Clamp it with the clothes peg.

3. Bend the pipe cleaner into a V. Put it in the clothes peg to make antennae.

4. Glue the googly eyes to the clothes peg.

Glossary

antenna feeler on an insect's head used to touch and smell

insect small animal with a hard outer shell, six legs, three body sections and two antennae

larva insect at the stage of its life cycle between an egg and a pupa; a butterfly larva is also called a caterpillar

mineral material found in nature that is not made by an animal or a plant

moult shed an outer layer of skin

nectar sweet liquid found in many flowers

pollinate move pollen from flower to flower; pollination helps flowers make seeds

pupa insect at the stage of its life cycle between a larva and an adult; a butterfly pupa is also called a chrysalis

Find out more

Books

Butterflies and Moths: Explore Nature with Fun Facts and Activities (Nature Explorers), DK
(DK Children, 2018)

From Caterpillar to Butterfly (Lifecycles),
Camilla de la Bedoyere (QED Publishing, 2019)

Life Story of a Butterfly (Animal Life Stories),
Charlotte Guillain (Raintree, 2014)

Websites

www.bbc.com/bitesize/articles/zwn6mnb
Learn more about life cycles.

www.dkfindout.com/uk/animals-and-nature/insects/butterflies-and-moths
Find out more about butterflies and moths.

Index